THE BOOK OF
SENSATIONS

UNIVERSITY OF CALGARY
Press

THE BOOK OF
SENSATIONS

Sheri-D Wilson

Brave & Brilliant Series
ISSN 2371-7238 (Print) ISSN 2371-7246 (Online)

University of Calgary Press
2500 University Drive NW
Calgary, Alberta
Canada T2N 1N4
press.ucalgary.ca

LIBRARY AND ARCHIVES CANADA CATALOGUING IN PUBLICATION

Wilson, Sheri-D., author
        The book of sensations / Sheri-D Wilson.

(Brave & brilliant series ; no. 1)
Poems.
Issued in print and electronic formats.
ISBN 978-1-55238-918-8 (softcover).—ISBN 978-1-55238-919-5 (PDF).—
ISBN 978-1-55238-920-1 (EPUB).—ISBN 978-1-55238-921-8 (MOBI)

        I. Title. II. Title: Sensations. III. Series: Brave & brilliant series ; 1

PS8595.I5865B66 2017   C811'.54   C2017-900386-0
                                                 C2017-900387-9

The University of Calgary Press acknowledges the support of the Government of
Alberta through the Alberta Media Fund for our publications. We acknowledge the
financial support of the Government of Canada. We acknowledge the financial support
of the Canada Council for the Arts for our publishing program.

Canada Council   Conseil des Arts
for the Arts   du Canada

Printed and bound in Canada by Marquis
This book is printed on Rolland Opaque Smooth paper

Editing by Helen Hajnoczky
Front cover illustration by Melina Cusano
Cover texture and ouroboros by Colourbox
Cover design, page design, and typesetting by Melina Cusano

For my mother and my father,
who bring me light and song;

for Leesha Withrow and Colette Mactaggart,
who assist and inspire;

and, as always, for poet, teacher, catalyst
Diane di Prima, who always reminds me
to be fierce—and to face the darkness.

Table of Contents

The Bibliobibuli

*Reading is the sole means by which we slip, involuntarily, often
helplessly, into another's skin, another's voice, another's soul.*

—JOYCE CAROL OATES

she gravitated
to the rarest book
lifted it, considered the title
without leafing
cracked it
open

ever after, she
never turned back
back—in double-time
fast track forward, the book
hacked into her life
24-7 27374
data breach, the book
took over
till she was out-of-reach
runaway addiction
text-book predilection
monopolization
go directly to bibliomaniac
do not collect $200

the craze forged fast
unruly bombast
blast off, ten times as fast
as a bullet, she's a bona fide

bibliobibuli, cool it!

doula of the tome,
can no longer focus on minutiae
so she loses her job
her relationship
her home—life in a shredder
becomes an open book

memento mori
hardbound is her verve
snapped between pages
of someone else's story
kinda sad
kinda sorry
kinda beautiful

in simultaneous time
once upon a—way back when
the end, never ends in her mind
it gets bent, hack attack spent
the end gets prolonged
horizontal as a logophile
librocubicularist, stuck
in a spine chilling position
between towering tomes

she's a bibliobibuli
letters, characters
become her only friends
as she can't make a versed amends
only a list of sadnesses
hamartia harmonized

sometimes
she speaks to the ink
in broken dialogue
tells it what she thinks
and when they reply
there's no punctuation
a nemesis' impossible situation

she'd rather read
a good love scene than have one,
bookmark the place, read a good meal
she'd rather skim the perfect twilight
than face the golden hour, imagine
catching stars in her hands

her reputation precedes her
a bad one—bacchanal
constantly drunk on volumes
and volumes of words
while the world gets bombed
on deception blues
she's chained to the chapter
of someone else's muse

before long she's abiding the binding
the older the better, bibliosmia
on this fetish tether, she's totally smashed
antiquarian aphrodisiac, she grows
into a hardened
bibliomaniac
wandering through an escapists'
simulation, over-stimulation of life
in a haze—she sees nothing, hears nothing
beyond the page

questions: did I read that
dream it
or make it up
maybe it didn't
happen at all

she's a notorious bibliobibuli
stuck inside someone else's lifelines
their breath, their ideas
she can't take flight, from the book
the astounding possession
can't put it down
click it off, or stop the reel

a bibliophilic bibliobibuli
a bibliophagist bookworm
bibliophile literarian, long term
bibliophily, her epeolatry legendary

not a case of epistemophilia
more, an escape artist's
hemophilia, her life
blood pumped of borrowed
ink, from a fount
that will eventually
run dry, meet another
end, an interloper
in her own life

she continues unidentified
lying in the fantasy
prone position
of a maladaptive daydream
or pedaling elliptical

into an infinite star stream

until she meets
too many of her own ends'
ends, end, fin
y diwedd
closing the cover
on yet another of her lives
she dies, she dies
so many times
she can't find the bottom
of her own grave

inter-ego-mortem
until she falls never ending
into a self-imposed
oubliette
taciturn

in her inky silence she thinks:
I could have been
a beautiful hat

Carded

card me please
give me a pass
and then, please
ask me to produce
the pièce de résistance
of Egyptian library cards
like the Royal Library of Alexandria
library card, or the Greek library card
to the Pergamum

apparently, they were dueling libraries
both vying for treaties
by philosophers and orators
both creating forgeries
to outdo one another
so what I'm saying is either library card
or both, undoubtedly of papyrus
my pass, my card, my ID

maybe
long lost to conquerors
wars and other tragedies
in the annihilation potpourri,
of faux pas fires, premeditated pyres
'accidentally' lit in the library
by Caesar, say
to piss-off Achilles
in 48 BC

passage please
allow me entrance
if for no other reason
than to decipher
the key to lost tablets
or to emancipate long
forbidden knowledge
from ash, cinder,
and the pickled brains of scribes

or, card me please and allow me
ingress to the Library of Congress
easy—way too easy

or please dear Michelangelo
grant me access to Library Laurentian
so I might reach into
the papyri, ostraca, incunabula library
encyclopedia knowledge embedded
below the paper line
a palimpsest maybe, or in a press-mark
seated at a pluteus, plutei grammaticales
yes, please spellbind me
in collections of recollections

or, card me please to the Ghent
open the cynosure of my eyes
to the all seeing tower of words,
as simple as clicking on an icon
of ten easy steps to Buddhism

card me please
give me access
bohoing praxis

present me
with a British Museum reading room
special research access library card
for scholars, a false respectability
as any stolen antiquity
take the Marbles, for instance

please give me first passage to walk,
I will walk the long hallway
towards your test room, authorization clearance
and you leave me alone to search
for the word 'Pythagoras' on your dino-puter
with an archaic bitmap font

I will search titles and call numbers
indexed in catalogues
to locate the spines
of rare texts on shelves
down some aisle
among millions of buried
well-hidden stacks
to prove I am worthy
of the esteemed pass
please library security
pass me—give me a card
for my pass—privilege
to call the book of my longing
to be delivered
to my own private pigeonhole

I know it will take weeks
to retrieve books,
deliver them to the Great Dome
weeks upon weeks

as the library overflow
spills deep into the tunnels
of the subterranean city
serpentine beneath
the hubbub of London town,
I imagine the snake of it
the long burrow of it
slithering reptilian domino
of uncharted books

I imagine
underground tunnels
of library books twisting
beneath Buckingham Palace
and The Tower,
filled to their rafters
with shelves, like underground shafts
lined with books waiting to be chosen
to be opened
and finally read

I imagine
the voices of books
as they begin to rise aether-like
as I walk above them
over London's cobblestones
envisioning what books
what authors
what thoughts
might lie below my steps
imprinted in stone
resolved, a little grey mouse
drives his little white lorry
around the coils, the tight roundabouts

of London to locate, little-known
Pythagorean titles, handpicked
from their catalogued-catacomb
the little grey mouse
faces the piercing eyes of the snake
to unearth the tomes
from their burial site

after weeks
of counting days
like abacus beads
the hardcover books
are exhumed from deep
in the subterranean city
and delivered safely
to central London

they are brought to me
at table #11
under the Great Dome
by a skinny grey mouse
in white gloves

I slide my fingers
and then my hands into a pair
of white cottons
gathering knowledge
serving my soul
think: Han Dynasty
library catalogue
scrolls of fine cloth
stored in silk bags

the skinny grey mouse
places the books
in my hands
at the heart of me
and for a moment we both
hold the books

I wonder if the books
have ever been opened
think: forgotten sarcophagus
ancient Egyptian quarry
converted archaeological dig

think: lost is
meandering between stacks,
titles blurring,
stumbling-upon a book,
the right book
is lost, like surfing the web
till you no longer
remember the initial word
of your search

back in Londinium
at table #11
I take the books
from the skinny grey mouse
under the Great Dome
inspired by the Pantheon in Rome
where all the greats deliberated—

Karl Marx sat in this oak chair
wrote the Communist Manifesto
Virginia Woolf perused dictionaries

in search of astonishing definitions
Mahatma Gandhi glided over
these floorboards as he contemplated
world peace; and the bookshelves,
shadowed bars where Oscar Wilde,
George Bernard Shaw, George Orwell,
Wells, Darwin, and Dickens scanned
for obscure titles,
and somehow they still hold court
circle overhead
like the ghosts of mouldy birds

ideas they were yet to have
still live in the crevices
of these walls—in the dust
of the Great Dome—along the spires
of the books yet to be opened

it reminds me
of a cathedral—where pillars
flying buttresses, still hold
the prayers of the souls
who worshipped there

and here, the residue
of secrets and inklings
in spiritus of great thinkers
link centuries
spin together, lifting higher
higher-learning, absorbing
knowledge by divine osmosis

I look down at one of the books
cobalt blue cover

between two white cotton gloves,
and carefully, in my hands
the hinge of the spine swings
as I open the front door of the book
and there, I check the sign out card—
how many times has this book
been signed out since 1740
only once, signed, only once
by, who—
it cannot be

I look around
no clocks
think: libraries
are like bars and casinos
beyond the confines of time

with the precision of a pick-pocket
I black-hole the heavy weight
paper sign-out card, between
the laminated library pass
and the plastic credit
in my breast pocket,
astonished, to have
a rare signature
over my heart
thunderstruck

flash! the cobalt book
in my hands
transforms into feathers
the feathers shape-shift
iridescent blue bird
red marking on zir crown

the size of a Macaw
ze returns my gaze
a familiar

zir abalone beak
mesmerising, our eyelids
blink, ornithological Morse code
I think: flight
of stares

ze flaps zir wings
and out of the feathers
the face of a human
becomes visible
ageless—diaphanous
pale with mauve eyes

I question reality
they dissolve back into
the book,
disappear

they say
if you see a ghost
and you question it
you will never see a spirit again

my mind returns to the library
still holding the cobalt blue book
I write a love letter to the library
which ends in a confession:
I won't return the books on time
they are lost
to the memory hold

Re: Reading

he reread the same book, never-ending
said he only wanted to read, or reread
one book in his lifetime—a page-turner
he was liber-monogamous

whenever he wanted to read
he'd buy a new second-hand copy
of the same title
over and over
carbon-copy chronicle

some kids want the same bedtime
story every night
till they know each nuance
by heart

but not this tsundoku,
his bookshelves were lined
reforested, spine-upon-spine
with the same vertebra
barcodes, vertical vertigo
different designs, different
type-faces

complete marginalia
abibliophobia free
still life, written across its jacket

some people collect
cork-screws and lotto-tickets,
airplane barf bags and geodes,
still, when does a collector turn hoarder
lectiophile turn bibliomaniac

fine-line turns grey area
life-line turns to tether
pillow, to asphyxiation

he slept on a blue dolphin bed
on the edge of nowhere
at zero gravity, he dreamt
he played a 40,000-year-old flute
he told himself he was well-read
but really he was well-reread
carpe librum librium
déjà vécu, drifting
on the edge of aubade

Dreams of Amaranta

they abandoned hope
of finding someone intriguing
to sit beside, split-second
double-take, wait

they spotted Amaranta
in the train window
her reflection superimposed
onto itself, ghostlike

they caught the sad woman
in an undivided stare,
her single-minded gaze

looking out at the platform
as if someone she loved
was standing there waving
good-bye, her concentration
piqued their curiosity
on the train headed east

if her stare was a color
it would be a rare kind of blue,
a sound, the echo shaped
by dead silence, a long track of blue
a despondent mood
the kind of blue that crushes
rock with shell, that impossible hue of blue
that sometimes protrudes
from the thin skin on the dorsal side
of an old person's hand
on a train headed east

they contemplated the twin vision
one real, one ghostly
double-edged—dreamlike,
she was a skeleton of sorrow
sad as a gypsy, a poet
someone who sees no tomorrow

they slipped into the seat next to her
like sliding along a wooden pew
asking: may I sit next to you

startled out of abstraction
she gave them the once over
and said: if you must, please do

they noted the fragility of her age
by the crackle of her voice,
she was the same vintage
as their Grandma the year she died
and yet, when they looked
into the train window
the reflection muted
almost erased her lines
of age, time disappeared

they noticed the beads
and hoped they'd never be forced
into wearing an idiot string
around their neck
to retain their glasses
like strings on mittens

that morning
there'd been a last minute

flurry to catch the train
now, a calmness descended
as the car clicked along
at a continual pace,
maybe it was the contrast
of the two, that made the day
move slower—
time extended itself
like in accidents or waiting
for love to arrive

they looked down at the old woman's
veiny hands—folded pensively on her lap,
held time like deserted sundials,
their mind somersaulted—came to land
at the bottom of a long hill
as they remembered, holding
their Grandma's hand at the hospital
as she released her life
and returned to spirit—

interjecting, she asked:
do you live in Portland or Seattle

relieved by the broken ice
they told her they were travelling
to Portland for a love interest—
which was a lie

there was a long pause

Amaranta imparted:
this is the first day I've spent alone
since my husband's funeral

they froze—observed
the tiny tic in Amaranta's eyelid
thought: we are so transparent
our bodies are constantly betraying us
transmitting messages
like Morse code

she said: it's best,
he had Alzheimer's—in the end
it was difficult

she reached
into her purse
pulled out
a white lace hankie
death aide-mémoire
thumbing the lace
she continued:
to watch a loved one dissolve
like a sugar-cube in hot water,
they die inch by inch

blank space fell between them

she expounded:
at first I could manage him
then it got worse, and worse—one day
I went to the grocery store
when I returned the front door was wide
open and the house was filled
with a thick cloud of black smoke
I couldn't even see the easy chair

there was a wild screeching sound
coming from the middle of the cloud
that's when my lights went on
and my Luis came into focus
he was in the middle of the living room
mowing the carpet—yes, he was mowing
our good Persian rug, the one we'd worked
so hard to save up for—and through
the smoke I could see
he was in a state of heavenliness
singing and giggling and mowing
the lawn, the carpet, the green

I started to laugh—I could hear myself
laugh over the sound of the mower
I yelled 'next time vacuum
the front lawn!' Luis looked
at me for a moment—we recognized
one another, and he turned the mower off
and we fell to the floor
killing ourselves laughing
like two children beneath a party piñata

Amaranta disappeared
she left them behind
on the train
to visit her dearly departed
Luis, for a moment

when she returned, she said:
now I can finally do
all of the things I've dreamed of

her eyes signaled grief
they asked:
what have you always dreamed of

silence collided

Amaranta burst into tears
she transformed
into a young woman as she cried,
she lowered her mask
so they could see what she looked like
before she lost the thread of her imaginings
for a twinkling, they saw her before
she was married, before she had children
through full-body-sobs she told them
she had no idea what her dreams were
now—she told them
it had been so long since she dreamed
she had forgotten how

they sat in her silence
until a breath of comfort
blew through them

without hesitation
they reached into their knapsack
pulled out a tattered copy
of Lorca's, *Duende*
they thought—this book has lifted
many out of depressions, they
thought—of the many cities and countries
the ragged book had traveled to
thought—of the impossibility of love
and the tenuous possibilities
of dream

they handed Amaranta
their prized possession
like a sacred offering

Amaranta said:
I'm not a book person

they thought—damn
I've already given her the book,
and their first impulse was to take it back
instead, they said:
please take it, and know
whenever you need to dream
you can open it and it will guide you
into your reverie

Amaranta lowered her eyes:
I shouldn't

they implored:
you must

I knew a poet once—
she said:
I knew a poet once

by the time they hit Portland
it was more like Portland was hitting them
with its sideways rain

Amaranta had released a little grief
like one wave breaks
on the beach, knowing
there's an ocean behind it

they had lightened their load
they didn't say good-bye
as they parted ways

∞

they left the platform
made a break for it
dodging the rain, took
momentary cover, beneath
awnings and trees,
the storm increased, the rain
was coming down in buckets,
they ducked into a doorway
spotted a sign—bookstore—a beacon
the opposite of oasis
they made a dash for it

a little bell jangled overhead
as they entered the bookstore—
inside soundlessness fell hard
and crashed on the wooden floor,
they scanned the space
all they saw was emptiness,
they thought—is this a post-reactor-disaster
ghost-town, like the abandoned city of Pripyat

dripping wet, they needed a private place
to take refuge, so they headed to the poetry section
at the back of the bookstore—the poetry section
is always at the back of the bookstore
maybe because it's the heaviest section
to anchor the books, in case of a twister

that day the poetry section
was a cheap motel, a one-hour room
poetry shelves were literarily jammed
with obscure and somewhat rare
new and used books—they sat
down to dry off, breathe, and take stock

they exclaimed: phallus of horses!
as they looked up
to behold the miracle, at eye-level
was the holy mother lode
of holy mother lodes,
it was a prophecy,
an infinite loop of allure
ad infinitum—their mind
Möbius, at the awesome sight
of an entire shelf lined with Lorca

—Lorca, Lorca, Lorca, Lorca, Lorca—
it was a picket fence of perfection
each vertical board, an obelisk

they guessed—a Lorca lover must have died
and left their corpus to oblivious relatives,
unwittingly, their kin dumped boxes
of priceless books at the front door
of the bookstore, thinking
the books were a burden,
the kin misread their fortune
and cast them out

finding the books
was like finding a Van Gogh
at a garage sale, a sunflower askew
in a cardboard box

they gasped: princeps of horrorificabilitudinitatibus!

why hadn't the booksellers caught them,
Poema del Cante Jondo—original edition
signed to Amaranta—*Romancero Gitano*—original edition
signed to Amaranta—*Sonetos del amor oscuro*—original
edition, signed to Amaranta—Amaranta—Amaranta

they thought they were hallucinating
at this antiquarian find worth a fortune
they looked to the corners for cameras
contemplated applying a five-finger discount,
even with slashed second-hand prices
the books were out of reach,
all they had was ten soggy dollars
in their pocket, and no plastic

the voice of reason/ unreason/ reason spoke—
don't do it—do it—don't do it

how the mind plays tricks
they considered—Lorca touched these books
he touched them, with his own genius
hands—the dust of Lorca still remains
in these books—
don't do it—do it—don't do it

his fingerprints are still
on these covers—I can touch him
through the marks
he left in the dust
between pages
his brilliance and passion
still alive in these volumes—
don't do it—do it—don't

Duende—lightning strike

they resolved to hide the books
somewhere inside the store
and return for them later
when they're flush

where—where would they hide them—
guided by the ghost of Lorca
their eyes looked skyward,
the voice of Lorca broke in already
translated into English:
hide me in the false ceiling

they wondered if the grade school time capsule
was still buried beneath the baseball diamond

their eyes landed on the sweet spot above
the stacks—they balanced on the stool
conveniently provided by the store
and hid the rare, priceless, signed, first editions
of Lorca inside the ceiling above
the ugly perforated tiles

that day, they placed more than volumes
of Lorca in a ceiling tomb

years passed
their mind often revisits
that treasure-trove
in the bookstore ceiling
and they wonder if they'll ever return
to retrieve their secret

they ponder
Amaranta's last words—
I knew a poet once,
I knew a poet once

and they wonder
if she ever found her dreams

The Smell of Old Books

pending rain condensed the air
in a pre-storm vice
no birds could be heard
a coffin with a tight fit, corpse rotting inside

peppermint pressed between fingertips
basil or lavender, honey
or sage, for that matter
the wing-dust of a moth

there once lived a shaman
who slept with his eyes wide open
and a lover who knew
her fertility cycle
by the scent on the nape
of her turned-on neck
catnip cackle berry
pheromones conspire
in the dark of night
cold to the marrow
clutching a seed pod of honesty
wool tweed of the old
country, damp in the new
grandpa always had one foot
in two worlds, never knew
how to integrate the scents
of two

after tobogganing
frozen hills, *ponaidah*
all a simmer on the stove

reminds us of his distant home
not matched by socks

olfactory flashback—
to the socks
the wool socks of a hitchhiker friend
who told me he hadn't removed
his boots in two months
wore them 24-7
in the swelter of summer heat

secondary olfactory flashback—
diesel in the hull
of a fishing boat, fills the blanks
of wanton bodies, musk of lovers
hours in, no end in sight, authentic
cooking in Katmandu not undone
by alligator stew, in the centre
of jazz blues, swamp of everglades
deep in the darkness of hidden caves
filled with bats, pine forest rain
forest cedar forest linking equators
tropical, bowl of sinsemilla, ounce
of isolation in a vial, scent of 1,000
books burning, fresh water
pond standing too long, bonfire
snared in a sweater, Lily the alley
cat scaling a building
to bring me a dead mouse
new baby, new car, new point shoes
new house, new carpet, new coffin
new book, face plant nose
in the crack of the spine, tears of sand
stone, octopus ink gem-drop, freshly pressed

anything, stitching, glue, resin
lemon, old musty words not afraid
of death, just being buried alive
unknotting flesh of outmoded suspense
these, are radical bibliosmia
        I simply remember my favorite things

the foreshadowing of death
is always life
        and then I don't feel so bad

back to the boot flashback—
he removed his crumbling boots
Chew-chew-knee my parrot
hooted, flew out of the room
as I threw the smell of him
off the balcony into a light blue
child's pool below, waiting
to be played in

new flashback—
old tomes engender new
satisfaction, old
volumes of folio olfaction
I start jonesing

find incunabula collection
entire room stacked and stocked
with scents of lost histories
exotic intoxication
biblical-stench blooms
so why not consider
nightshade suicide
armageddon petrified

grassy notes of arcane
archives, tangs of acid
hint of vanilla over
an underlying mustiness
mildew of erudition pangs
illustrious, as much a part
of the book
as its contents, inhale
vellum manuscript
new pulp fiction
deeper craving, wanting to believe
it's true as Rosa Calvaria
factious rose that wilts
into the shape of a skull
memento mori, petal head
folds itself into bone
labia in the face of death
pages like the skin of a ninety-eight
year old woman, posthumous
one-hour after
going to spirit

a certain hagiography
delivered by drone
was locked in a poison garden
for one last breath
of the parchment
holding a saintly darnau
of a cliff-hanger

Palabra Anteontem

no words
to describe
an imperfect
future, tense
rife with love

skewed
with super sensitivity

like a crocodile
cradles their fragile hatchling
between their teeth
to protect them

no words exist
that describe
deep feelings
only words
for sensations
seen in pictures
they fell out of usage

strange as a human who *meows*
to a cat, who doesn't understand *meow*
meow only sounds weird to the cat
I don't know how I know that
in the future cats teach me
to communicate with eye blinks   darllen rhwng

she put her cat eye
reading glasses on

to see the tacit leaves
of tasseography, cast
telepathically, which
happened to include something
about equinox eggs
standing on end

difficult to interpret
time flies, healing is slow
how do we find the words
when no words exist

The Booklovers

a eucatastrophe
or a dyscatastrophe, a catastrophe
are the same when you meet your end

the booklover
wails: it can't be over!—
throws the book across
the room, weeps:
it can't be the end,
it can't—damn you
damn you, damn you!

the booklover
feels jilted, wants to kiss
and make up or out
read something into rapt eyes
beyond the end, like a mummy
wants to continue loving
the daylights out of the book
but it's over

the booklover
lets out a mating call
so loud it reaches the Milky Way
river: I want more of you!—
but its over, over and out
hard to admit, to accept
still holding on to old ideas
like never-ending streams
dream of sipping elixir
from a bowl fashioned

in the shape of a dead
author's heart

this is the end, beautiful friend
the last word, the end
of life hurting more than death
the end, of long nights of openness
the end, of new chapters
this is the end of the line
the end of the long story
with twists and turns and wild demented songs
this is the end of allegory, I'm sorry
but this is the fateful end, beautiful friend
there are no more pages to turn
in the reading light

the booklovers body language
is a broken dictionary,
no skies or stars
or oceans or blood
just death, in two words
the end

long in coming
but shocking in its suddenness
last pages hit hard

no moon or sun or planets
or waves or temples or stones

the first kiss to the last
bookended, the finish line
no Spanish jasmine
just a white rose of sorrow

a eucatastrophe
or a dyscatastrophe, a catastrophe
are the same when you meet
your maker

A Word for Poetry

listen in
five elders of this land discuss
what the word poetry might be
in each of their languages

pause to bless,
to honour

one elder says: song bird
another: the sound of the wings of a small bird
as it lifts off the ground into flight

all feathers of rune
my heart cries
as another beat
opens
to an ancient song
anew

pause to bless,
to honour

they say, we're all born
with a song in our hearts
to tell us apart,
but we stopped
singing our songs long ago

born with a song
in the name of the language of earth
listen to the breath beneath knowing

pause to bless,
to honour

born with a song
to remember

Dreaming in Lost Languages

Bababadalgharaghtakamminarronnkonnbronntonnerronn
tuonnthunntrovarrhounawnskawntoohoohoordenenthurnuk!

—JAMES JOYCE

I like you better soul to soul
than in the fantasy
no time between our stars
please fly home to the river of life
with your haunting strings and searching guitars

I'm dreaming in lost languages

I like you better soul to soul
than in the fantasy
no time between our days
longing to touch your Draíocht land
from swerve of shore to bend of bay

I'm dreaming in lost languages

Gateways—
I like you better soul to soul
than in the fantasy
held between you and your guitar
I'm palpable tactility, with your obscure wings
it's your ways of being, it's your ways of seeing
I long for

I'm dreaming in lost languages

Awake—
Your hymn a wooden oath
two notes—betroth
as you strum your strings through my body
I feel you both
in this world and in the other—
outside the window
December night snow, falls
in little flashes
I unlock the hinge
to catch your slow motion stars
on my tongue

I'm dreaming in lost languages

Los lingos—
I like you better soul to soul
than in the fantasy
I'm river gypsy proud
of my own imperfect past
as I amble the labyrinth, of your limitless aftermath

I'm dreaming in lost languages

Away—
I like you better in the real
than in the fiction
something about the feel
in the flesh of my predilection
nostalgia speaks
the secret language of poets
for you—

You untie every knot of me
liquefy my philosophy, with your
deep song ecstasy,
the way you say my name
and talk to cats
with those long hooded eyelids
I'm missing you by miles

I'd cross the Golden Gate bridge
for one last breath of you
it's the things you see, I know
it's the things you see, I know
the things you see,
as the crow flies

You are mysteries unknowable
the stone tongues of lost sounds
idio-lingo
idio-lingo

Love Letters

… unless forgiveness finds its nerve and voice …

—SEAMUS HEANEY

And this is how the story goes, Fadó
This is how the story goes—

It's never too late for love
It's never too late to love

Years ago I had a boyfriend
Who wrote me slews and slews of love letters
He wrote me slews and slews of love letters
That I never opened,
I was way too busy for love
I was way too busy for love

So I never opened his love letters
And I threw his slews and slews of love letters
Into an old shoebox which I labelled 'later'
'Later,' an old shoebox I labelled 'later'

And then I put that shoebox labelled 'later'
Into another box, which I put into another box
Which I then put into a trunk
Which I put into storage in my parents' barn

It's never too late for love
It's never too late to love

Thirty years passed

I moved back home to Calgary
And my Mum said: Get your shit out of our barn

So I did
And I opened the trunk
And inside the trunk I found a box
Inside, another box
Inside, a tattered old shoebox labelled 'later'

'Later,' the old shoebox labelled 'later'
And I remembered later,
And I thought, now is 'later'
Now is 'later'

And I opened the shoebox, I opened my heart
And I opened the letters and I opened my mind
And I took time
I finally took time, for love

Slews and slews of love letters written to me
All those years before
I couldn't believe my eyes
I didn't know anyone ever loved me that much
And I thought of all the love
In all the shoeboxes, and such

So I looked up my old boyfriend on Facebook
And I got his number and I called him
And I thanked him for all his love letters
And we laughed and shared truth
And we promised to get together in the summer
For old times' sake
For old times' sake

It's never too late for love
It's never too late to love

Two weeks later, he died
And I was glad I had opened his letters
And finally took time for time

It's never too late to love
It's never too late for love
It's never too late
For forgiveness to find its nerve

Communication in Sensation
Cyfathrebu yn Sensation

this is a declaration of love, shamanist
in the lost name of a colour which no longer exists
in the language beyond words to express—

I stand breathless in the doorway
at the hospice, the portal to bardo
between the blurred lines of birth and death
in the place that holds no time
just Nain

my Grandma, Nain in Welsh
a hundred and one and a half
laughs in the face of her epitaph
and then asks me to join her
on her journey through death, cryfder
I say: absolutely—
yes

we begin
the dance of marwolaeth
we do not know the steps
and yet, we dance, we dance
ddaear y gwaed
as we live life Nain and I follow
the lines as they are given

we move forward
dip our toes into the other side
as if to test imaginations crest
like the Holy Head coastline tide

and then, we return to this realm
half glorified, to catch our breath
no time between our stars

we know we do not know where we are going
she reaches her boney hands
into the twilight hour, up, up
tells me: it's snowing, it's snowing—
I see her taste frozen light on her tongue
in a language betwixt and between

when I was young,
she taught me to tie my laces,
to tell time, and sound out each letter
now, she shows me how to walk through yn marw
and speaks in the language of soul

we share eyes, surrender control
and then we dance again
dip our feet into the other side
and return, again, fortified

next we go deeper into death
up to our ankles, our shins, our thighs
no time between our stars
until we are magnified Pleiades

we know where we are going
we are waist deep
and then, up to our necks
in death

Nain looks over and into me
with her final breath

and exits in a language of the sea
I know instantly, what she is saying
I don't want her to leave
I don't want her to leave me
she tells me mind-to-mind, to mind
it's time she goes on without me, hedfan fly
ffarwél

music of the unknown wonders cry
ffarwél, as she leaves her spirit with me
for safe-keeping
I hear a million hynafol voices speaking
in languages lost to my people
weeping, end of oak Celtiberian-ease
and stones, end of wind and bardic poems
crossbones scattered across the earth
in llwch i'r llwch, tones
ffarwél

to the natural world
word, lingua franca of birds heard—pictures
oneiric, names of ways of seeing and being
honeycomb—hieroglyphic pic's, alphabetic scripts,
all connected to this earth in metaphysics
musica universalis metamorphosis

symbols of symbols of cyphers of signs
coded in code encoded in storylines
love is a dangerous threat

glottophagy linguicide
when the last speaker
of a language dies

the last words of Nain
grow distant and pale
almost thin, they grow thin
as the human skin
one hundred years frail
becomes Cain paper
becomes a spider web thread
in the hail

sometimes I am the language
that just lost its last speaker
not misunderstood, erased
deleted by a friend
impossible to comprehend
maybe that is what leads me to poetry

the words of Nain
are distant now
thinner somehow

no time between our stars
naill ai

Naming it Ananizapta

when they say
say the magic word
to enter the secret passage
I imagine an oubliette

they say
intoned with spirit
any word might be magic
zebedee, zebedee, zebedee
maybe words ride the currents
of their own history
straight into transmutation

they say
don't say
the word
too soon

they say to say
the word first
then picture
the deed
is done

they say
magic begins
before the word
is said,
it forms
when the thought
is strongest

they say
that word's never been
deciphered, but
they don't know Hebrew
הטפז יניגע
interpret the root word
there—
the code is broken

∞

words are markers
evolutionary upshots
to name
in thought, sound, word
is to give definition
without explanation
no need to set in stone

if we erase the words
of the world, will we
give ideas new meanings

language is never complete
like a poem
always fluid, in motion
still searching for itself
undefined, evolving keywords
ongoing in process
of discovery, re—

a butterfly once
landed on my hand
beside the Elbow river

can't pin down
the nostalgia of flying
only build a language nest
one feather at a time

∞

naming words
to name more words
nomen nescio through polyonomos

they say
there is a supreme name
that will, when uttered
out loud, dispel
all danger

do you know this word
lingophile

if not, why
why not, why
has this word above all
been lost, and if this be
name calling,
let me call thee tacenda!

∞

as folklore's reduced
to a sound bite
advertising cable
television and hi-speed
connections

what happens
when poetry
becomes a buzz word
to sell cellphones

and how do we embody
the taboo word
that buzzes
like an errant judgment
through our blood

mosquito
for instance
scares me,
of being the last straw
to get sucked

like reading
about a virtual
reality app
in a newspaper,
only more
like a suicide
bomb

∞

collect your thoughts
your words

and place them
where the wind moves
where we swam in glacial waters

stories connect us
to place and displace
us and teach us
how to survive

imagine
being the only speaker
of a language

way of seeing
the last survivor
of genocide

to whom do you speak your truth

∞

we name, we name, and we rename
baptize
legitimize
categorize
capitalize
specified, we solemnize
to name something purple
to name something Cleopatra
to name something that turns old
I name this poem a list
I change my name
call it family Freud

using, over-using words
erases the first high
indulges the low
down, of meaning

change your name
change your face

every year Santa
would give me a silver dollar
to face my phobia and tell him
my most wanted list
he said: use your words

we choose tentative words
at funerals
everyone wants to be
the one most loved
by the person who died
hold your tongue
everyone dies too soon

found afloat
the dead were wearing
lifejackets, hanging on
to last words, like a language
lost, how do we make a list
when we don't know
their names

∞

no, no riposte
pauciloquent

word has it
it's just a wandering star
an egregore of trees, covered in eyes
migration of creation

half the time
I can't tell
if it's a flower or a weed
action of the phenomenal world
might be, let them all grow
words into letters into sounds

as green
as a Captain's log
signed simply,
–C

Language of the Birds

—Toni Morrison

gwawno gwawrio
gwawno gwawrio
gwawno gwawrio
I got up early that morning
before dawn, 'cause I wanted to see
the sunrise on Glastonbury Tor
and maybe experience a mystical moment
you know, at the Mists of Avalon, I don't know
I thought, maybe I could take a selfie

and there I was
at Ynys Wydryn, the Isle of Glass
before the sun rose
before the world awoke
en masse

the night before
Miss V, matron of the Air B & B
gave me hodgepodge directions
which I followed to the T

by rote she rattled off:
always fork to the right
the back way up Bove Road,
torque to the right of the fork
stick to the road along the fields,
twig right 'round the bend

second sign, fork right
dirt road, sheep in the lea,
she said, look for arrows
pointing to the T—to the Tor
furthermore, the third arrow is aiming
the wrong direction
go the opposite way,
when you reach the apple orchard
you've got your foot on the prey

okay
that morning I walked as I woke
preoccupied by the seven rays
I approached a large stand of trees
not mentioned on Miss V's mappish maze, maze
when a strange buzz filled the air
and an iffy breeze lifted, my malaise

suddenly there seemed to be a remarkable number
of birds flying over me
I looked closer, they were all crows, it was crazy
I'd never seen so many crows

and I thought, oh look
the crows came to greet me
at the foot of the Tor
for my mystical moment #metaphor
so I called to them: caw! caw! caw!
in West Coast Canadian crow
who knows what they thought I was saying
'cause they seemed to reply with a battle cry

my crow seemed to infuriate them
they started flying off the handle of their branches

supersonic wing and claw, they were
circling me like cyclones, livid and raw
the grove trees were covered in black feathers
instead of green leaves—ebony feather trees!

I didn't know what to do
so I decided to run like hell
and that's when I became their moving target
bombshell after bombshell
they were hurling twigs and little stones
screaming, dive-bombing and pelting me
like a garbage storm
in New York City

I screamed in the language of crow:
stop it! caw! caw! caw!
they thought I was saying:
bring it on mo-fo!

'cause that's when the crows
started poo-bombing me
first came one poo, then came #2
after #2—three—four—DEFEC8
in a 9.3 shit storm
early morning excrement blitz
the carrions were bombarding me
screaming, riddling and laughing at me
ha! ha! caw! caw!
they plastered me in their bastard
bunk, papier-mâchéd me in their fecal junk

I was running out of breath, and for my life
at that same time

poo running in my eyes
rendering me blind
gwawno gwawrio
gwawno gwawrio
gwawno gwawrio
it was a murder within a murder
of a million of crows, blithe-hearted
hanging onto the sky
of un-believability in high frequency
heaven knows

I don't know what made me stop
but I stopped
I stopped running
from the ravens, from the crows
of unrestful thought

wiped my face of corvus disgrace
and poof!
the incident ended as abruptly as it started
the crows were gone
and before long, I was standing
at the tip of the Tor looking down
on the Mists of Avalon
as the sun rose—in dawning dawn
I forgot to take my selfie
before me, there was so much more…

later,
on high street
a bell tinkled as I opened the door
and minding the hocus-pocus store
was a wand wielding witch

I asked:
what does it mean when a murder of crows
poops all over you

she said:
I thought you were wearing a hat
my dear, let me Google that
she searched—poop/ face/ crow

according to the website
and there is a website
when crows poo all over you
it's good luck, an omen, a sign—

I looked down at the poo
and said: excellent

she said: excrement
a crappy episode becomes
an auspicious payload
you're coated in a blessing's disguise

we cackled like a couple of old crows
word to the wise
gwawno gwawrio
gwawno gwawrio
gwawno gwawrio

moral of story—
when the world shits on you
let it be your armour of bliss

Re: Wyrd

back to the temple
it's time to go back in time
to change the flame
back to the fire within
back to the fire within
re: Wind re: Wild
re: Wind re: Wild
re: Wind re: Wild re: Wyrd!

sentenced to death for heresy
she was burned at the stake, as a witch
bird skull filled with red flight feathers
she was stoned to death, as a witch
capsized bottles of wishes
flesh-hook, worms and fishes; she was third-eye
beheaded, for being a witch, thrown
from a tower, defenestrated
in a hour-glass shower, of falling women
called a witch, a witch

a poisonous apothecary
scary, as a witch, hung by a rope, no hope
for being a diviner of fossils, onyx eggs,
bones, and rare shells—she was drowned
for sorcery, lycanthropy—called a witch, a witch,
a cunning woman, for sewing a severed head
with a cross-stitch stitch, she met the net of unfair
ends, by the dark of the moon
for kissing datura, for knowing the taste of apple
the eye of needle, the gaze of obsidian—a witch, a witch
for want of wonder, the church killed her

to erect Lady-shrines over Mother-temples
for the purse, the cathedral curse
for saliva of snake
she was burned at the stake
'cause she wouldn't obey, obey
she wouldn't, she couldn't obey

perish the thought
of paying to pray, as we become the prey
and our prayers become theirs
to sell back to us,
back to the temple
it's time to go back in time
to change the flame
back to the fire within
back to the fire within
re: Wind re: Wild
re: Wind re: Wild
re: Wind re: Wild re: Wyrd!

and her crime was—
she drank of clear waters
she drank the waters of clarity
and as she was the river
she was outcast, and I hear she wore
black clothing and odd costumes
she dressed in the hoots of owls
as Oak takes root, she howls
to the moon and the turning tide
of orgasms from steamy cunts
and wanton wombs, of horny eggs
in the fumes of sensual songs
of longing, plain as a leaf picked
from a garden surrounded by Yew

and pressed between her breasts
like a flower, dressed in striped stockings
with jeweled salamanders
in her hair, and oh the prayer
and oh the prayers
that killed her
as they killed her, again and again

back to the temple
it's time to go back in time
to change the flame
back to the fire within
back to the fire within
re: Wind re: Wild
re: Wind re: Wild
re: Wind re: Wild re: Wyrd!

Forest Bathing

there's more to a forest than trees—
arboreal salamander
red eyed frog, translucent as glass
whip-poor-will, chickadee
hornbill, toucan, hummingbird
yellow-bellied sapsucker, aye-aye
acorn woodpecker, sharp-eyed fox

there's more to a forest than trees—
scarlet tanager, buttercup
solitaire, chameleon, chipmunk, grey wolf, deer
flying dragon, lizard lord, iguana, dreamflower, newt
rattle bone, white stag, weevil

there's more to a forest than trees—
laughing owl, hoot hoot
omen rabbit, ladybug
black cat skull, skeleton bone, Lo Shu turtle shell
orangutan, bonobo, all alone in lingo
bluebell, bluebell
bird cherry, cherry

there's more to a forest than trees—
orb weaver spider, fungi, moss
monarch butterfly, beetle, honey-bee
earwig, ant, kinnikinnick, foliage bug, lunatic
gypsy moth, pseudo-centipede, lignicide

call me damselfly in distress
'cause I'm a wildlife worshipping zoetic mistress
tree hugging temptress, hemptress

it's all arborolatry to me

there's more to a forest than a tree

∞

I stand in arbor amour
in reverie, I deify all creatures in trees
the whole tree ecology, really
I can't just idolize one tree
must praise the whole arboricole

down on my knees, up from my root, I pray to trees
and meditate, as trees speak to me, and sing
in the wild of weald open wide world
the woods are quiet, but never silent

I cross over unfurled, and turn into
a full-bodied dendrophile—Daphne! Daphne!
the wind blows that curious way, up my bark
exclamation mark: I beseech you!

allow me to wade into the wilderness of you
slip into, dip into your fertile earth
and there let me bathe
in your girth, your grass, your sage
dear glade, feel the ring
of a thousand lifetimes in each line
as you turn my page, voice and music wed
tingling porcupines up my spine
all quill and musk, nothing left unsaid
by your erogenous breeze
if this be tree-gasm please
cwm/ cwm/ cwm, draconid, draconid

cwm/ cwm/ cwm, draconid, draconid
let us breathe together

allow me to soak in your woodland air
oxygenize, in a perfect photosynthesis
eco-erotic deliciousness—let me breathe
eternity—aerie of eagles
rustle through my leaves and needles
through the interwoven sticks of my nest,
as you saturate me
plunge me into biodiversity
please, let me breathe, in your families
of trees—dear forest—your chorus
sings in aromatic keys
all Ogham, shadow play
cwm/ cwm/ cwm, draconid, draconid
cwm/ cwm/ cwm, draconid, draconid
in harmony from floor to canopy

take me, as I take you—the way you are
humanity's pheromone labyrinth, please
splash me in old growth ecology,
in the deep sigh of phytoncide
slowly immerse my entire being
deep inside, till there's no line between you and I
merge and submerge
in each other's eyes
we don't disappear, but stay here
in a catharsis of true nature
cwm/ cwm/ cwm, draconid, draconid
cwm/ cwm/ cwm, draconid, draconid
forest green

you cleanse me
etch your initials on my body
back and thigh, invisible tattoo
ouroboros, snake and dragon eye—
look up to your branches, your sensorium crown
washes over, stillness, reverberates, undulates
cwm/ cwm/ cwm, draconid, draconid
cwm/ cwm/ cwm, draconid, draconid
you are every book I've ever read

∞

I've stood in a stand of many of you, trees
and taken a stand for your mysteries
I've slept in groves of ancient Oak, and dreamed
away lost sensations till I woke,
I've danced among Trembling Giants
it is told, all 47,000 Aspen trees in the grove
share a single root—and when we breathe
we breathe Quaking Aspens, 80,000 years old
in a breath of a billion leaves
in a breath of a billion leaves

in grief I've been held
in the arms of the hallowed roots
beneath Gog and Magog, among Mists of Avalon
I've made love against the moss of Carmanah
to belong, to the cathedral chant of peace,
and I have overheard Arbutus scream
as she peeled back her bark, and sang in a high-pitched
cry, source of essence
I have seen tears of the tree of joy in rapture
a deep song sorrow I cannot capture
unless I separate my heart

from knowing, I am human
as I long to belong with tree
bone and bole and bark and branch
in a shower of blazing stars, draconid
I've wandered, perambulated
botanical bohemian though Pines
and Firs and Cedars and Cypress
in the shivelight of Olive, Willow, Ash, Ginkgo, and Yew
of Bodhi, Baobab, Redwood, Rowan, and blue Birch
as they died and as they grew
in my search, my endless search
for aeaea—aeaea—cwm/ cwm/ cwm
draconid, draconid
albino raven galw/ galw/ galw

today, we plant a tree
for generations, divine meditations
to breathe—
a forest takes centuries
to breathe—
there's more to a forest than trees
we plant—we breathe—because of trees
we plant—we breathe—because of trees
we plant—we breathe—because of trees
centuries, through
centuries

∞

a tree
does not a forest make

I have heard it takes
one-hundred years
for a tree to speak or listen

or susurrate in slow-mo frisson
trees breathe at the speed of healing
slower than a stand-still
slower than a grain of sand
holds a single ray of sun
entranced, slow as nematode

trees are special that way
they take a long time
to know,
and so do I

when I finally
returned to the forest
where I learned to love so long ago

the forest was gone
cut down
to the ground, no tree spared
and all that was left

were twigs, debris
and the hollow echo
of wind
tumbleweed

everything else had died
and I realized

there was nowhere
to turn, nowhere to run
to hide

Interview with Ocean

Why do you look at me that way

    your movements are a language
    unto themselves, I want to know you
    become fluent in every nuance
    of you, rhythmical in you
    no two words, like no two waves,
    are the same, I want to learn
    every meaning of you
    every twist, turn
    every—one/ two
    one/ two—of you
    quiet in the wild, weightless
    and demanding, leaping and flying
    diving and landing, your movements
    are a language unto themselves
    eloquent, sonic haptics
    57 octaves below middle C
    in a dialect of darkness, euphonic
    your body orates
    beauty rare salutations

That's a lot to take in—what do you want of me

    I can't look away from you
    from your intrigue
    your unresolved mystery
    like death, cerddoriaeth yn gyffredinol
    between syllables of longing
    difficult to comprehend

oscillating breath
with each of your tides
the earth inhales and ex–
your movements
are a language unto themselves

I consider stars
alive on your rippling skin
like satellite vision
imagine the sounds of Draco
Javanese gamelan of cat's eye nebula
alive on your rippling swathe
a meteor shower, sparks of tailings
alive on your surface tension
the tip of your tongue
an unnamed gesture of your hand
Isadora swaddle to shroud

What do you speak of

dreams, legato
it is said there lived a dragon
named Ladon, with synesthesia
serpent insight
who guarded a tree
of golden apples

apples, like life stars
undiscovered constellations
colours reflect feelings
the gravity of opulence

like Ladon you are moon tied
gifted with extra sensibilities
and yet, held by garrulous silence

in my dream, my dragon dreams
in the language of your movements
azure blood breaker to briny sea, fluid
in the—one/ two
one/ two—of you, of me
Isadora swaddle to shroud

Yma fod dreigiau

the language of your movements
guided by wyvern bioluminescence
the deep-sea killer who will not live
in captivity, would rather die
than be caged by the question
of what their deep-sea eyes have seen
so adapted to darkness, they are blind
to light

I cast-off your power
illusive as an attack
from a prehistoric shark
with three hundred rows
of needle-sharp teeth
sinking in
the birth of your flow
from erupting volcanoes
crashing comets

Where does life begin for you

in you, Ocean
life begins in your salt
and now, your fatality is my fragility

Come to the edge of me—feel my tide on your toes

> I fear you as I respect you
> you dragged me under
> took my breath, blood vessels burst
> in my eyes, in your crescendo
> you grasped my neck, held me
> under, in a strangle hold close enough
> to death, to hear the rattle of rale

I do. I did. I will. Your bones remind me of coral

> with graviloquence
> your thermonuclear bomb of elemental blue
> menaces around me, I whorl through
> spin into you, dizzying me
> lightheaded I open my body
> buoyant shredded—on, in, through you
> your waves rock-bottom me
> throw me against a million shades of blue
> a Jackson Pollock magnum opus
> akin to looking through
> the astonishing eyes of peacock
> mantis shrimp, bulging out of ultraviolet distortion
> and it is impossible to calculate your age
> and yet, your language so new to me

Shall I sing to you

> yes, sing high fidelity
> through green in blue
> sing paradox, in lingua enigma
> I cannot name this feeling of blue
> so I cannot tell if it is true

if it exists at all
at the speed of sound
you stroke my hair
I know naught what I speak
so I hold one drop of you
Ocean, like a long lament
one droplet of your salt
on my fingertip, and listen
in silence and awe
as you rise to meet your end

When you leave, will you carry me with you

I will float on your tears
tens of hundreds of millions of years
until you drown me in your loss
until your sounds shudder
through my bones

Eventually the world catches up with memory

thank you for getting back to me
for agreeing to meet me
I know you are busy

What is true

pieces of disappearing poems
fit to be tied, I look
at what my people have done to you
and I am sorry, sorrier than a sentence
could express

pieces of disappearing poems
I am sorry, as I revere
your noble turns, crests, kelp, krill
and riptide, ray and reef
there live so many lives beneath
the surface of you, like dreams
all night, night sweats

pieces of disappearing poems
I know so little about you
your uncharted depths
I am sorry
for what my people have done
primordial Ocean
you do not deserve
what we have done
I cannot pinpoint when
unconscionable acts became
conscience acts of destruction

∞

It is too late to learn a new language
You cannot capture me with words

In sweet naivety, you also perish
Ask your readers: What kind of suicide is this

Your blood is made of mine
You smell and taste of me
Your veins ebb and flow with me
As do the moon and fertility

When you cry for me, you cry for yourself
And as your tears enter me, my waters continue to rise
You drown in your own sorrow

The day will come when you will return
        from whence you came
Nothing will be left behind to remember you,
        except—a feeling lost
        to you

Voicing Many Languages

in the language of dreams
oneiric flowers of milk and honey
sing like water

       would you drink wine with me—
       old world or new
       would you crack open
       that 4.5-billion-year vintage
       sealed with wax
       full-body bouquet, sepulcher-cellar

       and drink with me to the backstory,
       to the excavation, of wine bottles discovered
       in a tomb of two sarcophagi
       one holds the body of a man
       the other, the body of a woman
       they say the wine was provision
       for their celestial journey,
       and of the ten vessels
       found in the dead man's sarcophagus,
       only one still contained any liquid—
       my guess is, he made it
       wherever he was going
       with wine to spare

       my original question to you,
       will you drink with me—
       in the name of Dionysus
       ayahuasca, peyote, mescal
       in the name of wormwood
       in the name of climate change

having a universal meltdown
in the name of the newly discovered
30,000-year-old virus buried
in Arctic permafrost
in the name of unmarked nuclear
waste burial sites, and collisions
of omnipresent space junk
in name of entomology
of body language
dancing across blue annoyance
ascending and descending
clouds are stories without words

in a language without an alphabet
threatening cumulonimbus

will you drink with me—

in the language of sea, shells her megaphone
she speaks transcendent in the language
of survival and whistling and gesture
in the dystopia, whirling around
first speaker, last, last speaker, first
how do we converse, traverse
commune in a first language, through
to the last, in the language of soul

will you drink with me—

in the language of the movements of people
to earth patterns

in the language of poverty
epilogue of the day-in-day-out slog,

so close to the end we can taste
the cemetery air, the bone-rack rattle
of hunger's despair

they say money talks
in fact, it screams:
coin that, patent
the copyright
watermark the waterline
monetize, and then in an
instant, wash it away

> if you want me
> come and get me
> I am stuck on the other-side
> of this spider infested crawlspace
> cocooned in a tattered blanket
> of my dreams

when trees speak, they wail:
don't cut us down
to line your wallets,
cash and toilet paper
it makes no difference
if you take my life from me
stock, stop quomodocunquizing
we hold the medicine of your survival

> two bytes worth
> crypto currency

drink with me—
in the language of tarot
where there is no future
except to the charlatan

from logophobia to verbomania
and every cluster-fuck in between
is the language of love,
letters shaped like a Koon balloon
punctuation of a Haring rebel heart
fractal latitudes, miraculous-attitudes,
rwy'n dy garu di, and others
amaranth, as an imaginary
flower that never fades

devotion returns in hiccups of ambrosia
in the immortal language of flowers

        five red tulips in clear vase, posits:
        I'm a ten-dollar bouquet
        ripped from the earth
        deracinated so, in a sense
        I speak to you of love
        even as I long to live

        a handful of pennies
        obsolete copper coins
        drop into my water
        they settle
        weightless as a wish
        in a futile effort
        to save my wilting body

        for a moment, I breathe
        return vertical, knowing
        I will bow to gravity
        without a breath, or good-bye
        this is how the world will end   liber floridus
        not with a bang
        but a whither

in the language of soul

      never use the word soul in a poem
      will you drink with me to that, to—

hand clapping flamenco, cries of the heart
spinning duende, tension taught
as the animal slayed by a poet's knife
pools of blood and pails of tears

the colour of ruby

        to the heart of Barcelona
        I took flowers for the fallen
        killed by firing squad, bomb blast
        after fascist bomb blast

        in the heart of Barcelona
        I took flowers for the fallen
        to the enclosed square
        where bullet holes
        line the stone walls
        like execution pock marks
        scars of a broken prayer

        and when I was there
        the invisible hand of a child
        still at play, ghost laughing
        yanked the thin strand
        of ruby-red beads
        from around my neck

        in the heart of Barcelona
        the beads of my ruby necklace

burst and sprayed
all over the gothic stones
on the ground
like a million
beads of
blood

all around,
for an instant, I heard
a hail of bullets

I bent down
and placed my flowers
155 roses,
flowers for the fallen
on the ground
over the site
where my ruby
necklace
cried,
for mercy

please drink with me—

in the language of birds
in the language of ocean   speaking moon tongues
in the language of grain   in sunflower seeds
in the language of perspective
                through the lens of an unknown artist
light refracted in rainbows
of wavelengths,
let me buy a vowel

and let us drink—

they say, sunflowers say 'summer'
like nothing else
call it a verdict, sentence, prognosis
in the language of a death, doula
time is of the essence, acceptance
of a death sentence, terminal
life sentence, our appeal

> I was very young
> when they told me it was lights out
> there were no more flowers

in the language of prayer
speaking to the gods, or begging them
to see moon blood, flush the flower blush
or listening in to the gods in meditation

> listen in as the loops
> unravel, awaken as the
> stars rain downwards

> will you drink with me, please—

in the language of soil
communiqué of préservation
or destruction

> what is a symbolic act

petroglyphs and hieroglyphs
architecture and artifacts
all told history
memories grounded
in ancestral connections

earth, language, sound
the first cry of a babe at birth
civilization begins
with a single breath

as language melts away
so do the words for snow

in the language of deep listening
sign of a single breath
breathing though the entire body
of thought

in the language of knowing
without the need of words

     will you drink with me—

in the language of programming
of hack, spoken on line

     will you—

in the language of the blues
in the language of the street
slanguage—rhythm of the beat
depends what rue you're walkin'
will you drink with me, my friend

     I hear Ted Joans, say:
     jazz is my religion

yes it is, yes it is
will you toast with me—

Dear 14 Immortals

high in your castle tower
feasting on pheasant under glass,
you choose our words carefully
for on-the-grid (g)lossaries
filled with startling expressions
first straws, and last impressions

dear 14 immortals
whatever words you decide
survive, but
words are indelible
formed from the vernacular
of the people, they emerge, happen
they arise

whatever words you accept as new
will be the words people use,
yet the words you ordain
are the words we already use,
and who chooses you to choose our words
who elected you immortal

please, adjust our immovable eyes
break the rules, feel the darkness
or a sinking cry, and why not
accept the word librocubicularist,
it will happen whether there's a word
for it, or not—people will continue
to read in bed—fall asleep between
covers spilled open to receive

the altered reality, the gibberish
of their somniloquy

dear 14 immortals
what words will you accept
what will you reject
what is your post-truth criteria
lexicographers extraordinaire

do you keep up with technology
what will you re-reselect, re-eject, re-reject

the bigger question
would you choose
to have a permanent tattoo
of the word obsolete
inked on the posterior
of your criteria

signed,
scrabble

Conlanging

Invent a new language anyone can understand.

—Lawrence Ferlinghetti

pick the brain of Conlanger One
plant a plastic eye-catching flower
on the lip of neologism
script-tweak, hexspeak, leetspeak—31337
this is not a fire drill
it's not a symbolic security breech
so keep your data safe
bury your passwords deep
in a safe or on the cloud
cuckoo land, if you dare
this lingo-virus bares crossbones
results in the green screen of death
stark as the marrow of ancient ways
disconnect if you have to, hibernate
from the anonymous black hat hack
rewire your mother tongue
download your life on a shiny
black external hard-drive
call it your personal black box
thanks for the memories
not so far-far-flung, stop waffling
you know you've already been hacked
turn chronos to kairos
3-2-1 times up!

pick the brain of Conlanger Two
the creator, of java code
standard library—no card needed

yo-yo between unalike environments
test and debug
test and debug
break it, verify it works
across scores of browsers
so to speak, in the lingo
of compatibility, of high-security
and low vulnerability
clock-in, clock-out, beat the clock
in code, in binary, in techno-talk

this new language
must be simple, object-oriented, familiar
must be robust and secure
must be architecture-neutral and portable
must execute with high performance
interpreted, threaded, and dynamic

```html
<!DOCTYPE html>

<html lang="en">

    <head>

        <meta charset="utf-8">

        <title>Minimal Example</title>


        <script>

            window.onload = function() { //This function
starts after loading page

                document.body.appendChild(document.create-
TextNode('Hello World!')); //body element declared latter


//but code will be executed after page is loaded

    }

}
```

pick the brain of Conlanger Three
vintage triple nine society
take the tutorial
learn the neo-language
before it's too late and obsolete
stay ahead of neo-cartography
get a dream job in A.I.
lead the brain machine
(I mean team)
into the art of artificiality
feel the artificial breeze
pick the artificial flower
turn 180° into unreality
false news blaring
on multiple tvs
start a fake fire
in your artificial heart
with your manmade skin
and faux smile, it's time for your artificial
insemination widdershins,
the free range invasion
knowledge engineering 101
has taken control
smile you're on candid camera
robot—bleep, performative
damnatio memoriae

who invented latin anyway

pick the brain of Conlanger Four
let's converse, cool as a cucumber
created a wholesale language
was the linguist hired
by the movie industry

to write a language for aliens
to speak, and now the film company
is the proud owner
of the creator's words, and his way of seeing
makes him a third-party player
in his own life, he made a language
for actors to speak
full of fabricated life
not passed speaker-to-speaker
generation-to-generation
only line-to-line, script-to-script
stand-in-to-stand-in
body dust to body double

who owns a word like 'three-peat'
coined by one, trademarked by another
three-peat, three-peat, three-peat
should I patent a poem
can words be owned
open source

stay ahead of language
instead of beneath it
read the signs, they say:
bears are not allowed at the garbage dump
and somehow the bears know
to beware of human waste

let me know
the location of the shallow trenches
of radioactive waste-storage
the burial sites, so I don't disturb the curse
of the Pharaoh, so to speak
the tomb of the ancient Egyptian

sensitive information wiki-leak
who do we call before we dig
message in a bottle
buried by the immensity
of the sea
how does the future read
maybe on a clay tablet
of over-carelessness

do we ask ourselves,
is this an atomic proposition—
am I an adoptee of the parse tree
syntactic structure of a sentence—
I say, eff-that

wonders never cease
how many times have we changed
the seven wonders of the world
but what are the consistent wonders
list your answers in alphabetical order
type them on phonetic keys
find the best text-to-speech site
(with a natural sounding voice)
for free, hear your answers
played back to you

pick the brain of Conlanger Five
translated concepts instantly
automaton-to-automaton
machine-to-machine communiqué
secret lingo of an android
assembled as a fictional humanoid
then ask yourself, will we all be emojified
reduced to a series of pictograms, sound bites

how do we think once acronyms are reduced
into a language of micro-substitutes
pac-man just chewed that idea
and spit it out in pixels,
into the mire of the deep web

silence is not golden
where we live, rat-a-tat-tat-tat-tat
there's so many layers of noise
we can't reach the centre
of the enormous 4-inch jawbreaker
candy ball of constant clatter
colloquial speech

let us reread flowers in the wild
(sorry, there is no wild)
let us reread Ogham leaves in trees
(sorry, there are no trees)
let us reread lines into ants
cutting across the dust toward dirt
on their underground uphill grind

if we listen, we'll hear the sound
of glaciers melting, mais oui
we'll read each other's shortness of breath

we will read each other's shortness of breath
when we think of crowds, crowding us
with funding, sourcing, surfing, killing
let us consider outsourcing the idea
see if it returns into the language of Oc
see if it stops
the screeches of artificial speech
sine-waves for culture hacking

pick the brain of Conlanger Thee
clang your head against an open loophole
of creation, lingua ignota, to add definition
build your own alphabet
ergo lingos logos, bend sound
barriers into meanings that wander
aimlessly, who will speak
thee, who will speak to
thee, who will speak thee
who will speak to thee, who
will speak thee, who will speak
will speak to thee
if none, do you exist

I ask my shoes
are you the misfit or am I

I sing a lullaby
to language after languish
as they die
new ones arrive
sing a lullaby
to a new language
I cannot understand
life undecipherable
as a duet of birds

Scandalous Women

anthro-surrealist
graphic Penelopes

open your secret faces
de-petal the final rose
randomly mount
unrequited demands
and be love

re: ed

really, para-eroticism
is mechanical anatomography
so revolt and survive page 227
laden with hostile inter-body edification
look elsewhere
be bad—make itself yours
of love, yours, as it is: the
of the you; and the
of

love, erotic
would be a corporal life app,
with trans-privet swollen positions
bodies thrust red, and enriched with longer
twitching, with fuse of faces
lines, and nervous text
like: in, ed, di, if, or, of
as you strive toward
one-ism, why not
grant black sun societal love id,

discover pendant clasp
un-become a force of law
erotic with, lovers

elementary deduction

love upon the plane
of every erotic breath

L' Alcôve

*I always imagined I would have a life very different from the one
that was imagined for me, but I understood from a very early time
that I would have to revolt in order to make that life. Now I am
convinced that in any creativity there exists this element of revolt.*

—Leonor Fini

L of opening
hidden behind eyes
beneath her palpebral drapes

she shared her body's
aphrodisiac thought patterns
cut with pinking shears
to disguise her torso
tight with corset ties

she was taken underwater
preferring to walk alone
concealed under a mechanism of dream
cardinal anthropomorphic
demimondaine metamorphic
hers an apotheosis
a conservatory for lovers
sphinx body

the cover of every book
that spent time in the sea
I started reading her at the ankle
bone, and continued up her leg
to her subconscious

she died the day I arrived
to relive her fiction
she offered me lifelines
as I drowned in her reverie

not quite nice—
a cat caught in a tree
in anarchy, in branches
of ambiguity

just always had
an affinity with
Fini

Exploration of the Source
of the Orinoco River

after Remedios Varo

If captains of ships
are philosopher Kings
then what is the skiff herself,
as she opens her wings
to the wind

We know she knows
the depth of water,
as her telepathic body
cuts Adam's ale in two,
three, she glides between motion detectors,
concealed in her red ovum dinghy,
she swirls between worlds
above undertows,
a stationary gravitational slingshot
in slo-mo, she dares democracy to let her go
back, to free her from exile
back, to tributaries she no longer knows

So she sources the source,
finds the hollowed tree
where sits the holy grail—filled with her own making
and overflowing into the river on which she travels,
dressed in a stylish escape valve
a refashioned waistcoat
designed to look like a tub boat,
she floats

in her vessel,
her capsule,
her basin,
her canvas

Concurrently
she is left to her own devices
she invents a contraption
assembled for her own navigation
by a thread, with strings attached, she is fit
to be tied to herself, in order to guide
herself, parachute or plug—
she'll be prepared to pull the chord
untether herself, make a break for it
into her ignis fatuus maybe—super REM

'Cause she's a true Orinoco oneironaut,
she looks down at her compass
instead of the face of her,
for she is an organism spitting her own course
she floats, through a flooded forest
of death, looking for life
looking for fallen angels
on which to pin her scarlet wings

She tips her doodada bowler,
knowing she's already transformed
into a golden snail,
and the paint on the picture
is the home on her back

Her boat speaks:
I am the contraption
of your own making

She replies:
Confine me as you define me
cadavre exquis,
and know, I know
the birds are watching
because I drew them there

Now—
let us do the anaconda

Drones Kill

I guard the deep ID of my inner id
amid invisible lines on a neon grid
buzzing overhead, severing the sky
aerial robots with the bloodshot eye
of Sauron, of so long, of no long good-byes
of another apple-less piece of Miss American pie

and they say one drone's a spy—5,000 feet high
while another one kills without questioning, why/ why/ why—
'cause the pilot's remote, and widgets don't hear the cries
of children at school hit by Hellfire flies,
of a hostile hi-tech missile.

And in a warzone of droning-drone-drones
is a classroom which is filled with firing tears
instead of shooting stars and spinning spheres
and wishes, tingling with tadpoles and fishes,
and rhizome dreams—
while back at home in a Vegas strip mall
hi-tech fan boys don't hear the screams
as they perform video game drone-strikes
slurping coke, eating chips, and searching for viral memes

Bazinga!
The drones that walk—and talk and talk and talk
drone on about peace, but there is no cease-fire,
as they target practice, with so-called surveillance apparatus
artificial intelligence with security clearance status,
and they're calling it a covert smart/ smart/ smart drone,
like downloading an endangered animal ringtone
on your disposable smart phone for free—

it's a totalitarian parody
ignis fatuus homeland security
will-o-the-wisp, fatality after fatality after fatality

A sales rep drone circles for another pass
and I hope I'm not being paranoid about the asteroid
but really, there's no way home,
as I speak in a superflux of this recceing drone
with 20-20 vision—and facial recognition
of our bones and our chromosomes
which hovers above, scanning and gauging us, dystopian
draconian, as mechanisms replace organisms
and our behavior patterns reduced to predictable algorithms
credit ratings, purchase records, filter bubbles—
phobias, hang-ups and emotional troubles
are all known by the mighty surveillance drone
and the drone drones, as if to say:

We know what you want to buy
by the glint in your eye
don't worry you don't have to be home
we'll deliver your package from Amazon
tomorrow by air drone

Who's the user now
replace the word it with thou,
gods forbid we can't just disallow
a potential cash cow—overhead is over-overhead
as Fahrenheit 9/11 reports a newfangled gun
and the old peeping Tom is now carrying a bomb
for social media and the pentagon
who conveniently call drones UAV's and RPA's
next they'll name them 'flying cabarets'
while Orwell staggers in a scopophiliac haze

don't say the D–word—drone/ drone/ drone
don't say the D–word—drone/ drone/ drone

drones kill the birds and the bees
as they become voyeurs in all of the trees
paparazzi in parentheses
they collide with airplanes and screw with disease,
as they shrink in size, they'll be micro-Mordor-articles
small as gnats, like tiny flying god particles
more and more difficult to detect
as it becomes harder to trust and connect

Drones circle for one last pass,
as off-the-grid living writes its epitaph,
along with airspace, and Merlin's staff,
the sea fortress and the holy grail,
and—

all that's left is dead nightingale, or to
find someone to love
look them in the eye
and see their soul
celestial and whole
and know we are home
sometimes, we find our way home

Natural World of Languages

the language that granted
us safe passage
is gone—lost to the placebo night
of greed, to the continual fight
of spend, spend, spend to the end—to speed
to personal gain—the more mundane
beige, to the torment cage
community behind bars of material
waste, unhallowed ground free-based
country killed by its own security
safety trigger—bang—another gun
goes off untraced, invincible
as a militant group, hopped up on
Captagon—another gets erased
attack after attack laced, up the ying-yang
with no vision, another war drug of choice,
another, colour collision, and we're losing it all
we're hiding behind a smuggling smirk
of quick click conceit—the gimme
gimme, gimme—gormandized elite
narcissistic, ego-arsonistic
post-after-post—like, like, like
like I'm all out of like—scoring dope
is another nothing, from the info ghost
while books are burned
and our ruins are toast

∞

what was I going to say
the cure capsule's on the tip of my tongue
standing with the lights out
in the dark before the storm
its' difficult to swallow

allow me speak in plain slanguage
a language writing itself

we've been living on straight jacket luck in a kismet suit
forbidden fruit petrified in a permanent salute
of genocide, simulated unnaturally domesticated
born of seeds from a black market stall
while time for sharing
had its day at the mall
noise, noise, noise—
advertising everywhere
spam, junk mail, pop-up
buy me, sell me, buy me, sell me
selfie, love me, selfie me, me
me, me, meme, me, mine me
emoji, pre-fab brain circuits
it's all news and noise
news and noise to me
me, me, me, me, me
you tube you
you on the tube

loud, pathetic as apathy
we don't look each other
in the eye, anymore
mystified by our own self-images,
by our selfie cells, selves, sell, sell
we don't look at the world

around us anymore
even in the face disaster
it's a candy store of death
taking/ making video
of the here ever-after
posting it live, live, live
blood on the street, hands
live, live, live, life

and how do we erase
a public hanging shown as news
or the moment a suicide bomber's
shot, rolls over, pulls the pin
blows himself into smithereens
and then blasts it across our screens
an airport, ripped threadbare,
a night club dance of despair
or the street carnage of a celebration
how do we find peace

look into a techno window
world of arrows, pause bars
instant re-playback payback
conned, we're being
photo-bombed by a real bomb
of terror, into panic button culture
vultures

till there's nothing left to breathe
and if you talk about it
you're told they've won,
but taking time to grieve
makes us human

how can you care about the life
of another, when you don't even
care about your own

there's no scare there
there, scare

∞

lost is the natural world of language
in green idioms, etymological meridians
of earthen ley-lines, crossing crosses
beneath our feet
un-syllabled sounds of ancient myth
truth of stone written hieroglyph, when
we finally tell a different story
change the time-worn oratory, allegory
we'll create change
when we take time to listen
listen, we might be astonished
what we're able to hear, like
we're in this together
like it or not
bookmark that thought

∞

lost is the natural world of language
premonition, intuition, incantation, invocation
lingo of crow Shinto, antediluvian vowels

search—a word that means without words
find—there isn't one—no word for no word
the closest we get—heb eiriau

which asks
how would you like to be buried
'cause if we're not together in life
we'll surely be together in death

what do you say
when you approach a person
who is under the vow
of silence
a word is a nod
in reverie

∞

when was the last time
you heard the rare language of earth
untouched by human hand
with not a trace of passage
as rough and raw
as when the ground was made

when was the first time
you heard this earthly selenographer
sing praise to the moon
from the middle of nowhere
craggy and wild, or beheld
the birth of a bee or a bird
heard, the sounds of the long forgotten
stories of sky, awyr mine
stars speaking moon
the music of the spheres
astronomical, when was the last time
we could speak of our fears
or hear the wind

∞

the wind (whistle)
one day on the way to school
I stopped to listen to the wind
and the wind told me
it would be alright if I was late
the wind wrapped herself around me
and told me to resonate
to create, the wind whispered
sounds of beauty in my ears

at school, I was sent to the office
I told the principal
I was listening to the wind
and I told him
the wind told me
it was okay
to be late, the principal tried
to give me the strap

and that's when I learned
the wind is difficult to trap
he tried to give me the strap
I pulled away
pulled away
pulled

he hit the desk
until he was sorry

I say, this is the way
the language of birds

is forgotten
one story at a time

for
we are told
we cannot listen

for
we are told
there will be
consequences
if we listen

in the name
of language dreaming—
stop—
look—
listen—

to the language
beyond words

to the language
beyond words

to the invisible language

word

Sound Swept Away

synau ysgubo i ffwrdd
inside the covers
of a worn and weather-beaten book
where each line is red flagged—

there lives a tattered tale
of recluse Hikikomori
Hikikomori, by any other name
knows we will all be alone
in the end

∞

synau ysgubo i ffwrdd
later
I met a level 4 Klingon speaker
in the gender neutral washroom

with only a stall wall
between us
we spoke

in unison we said
nomen nudum
punch buggy

in concert
we flushed
in chorus
I knew it must be love
at first respite

in chorus
we spoke the same
non-sense, unnamed

∞

I pulled the card
from my breast pocket

∞

we are seeds floating in coracles
through acres
of clouds
looking down
on surrealistic seas

∞

synau ysgubo i ffwrdd
going through her things
we found
a scratchy letter,
grandpa to grandma—
proposing marriage
tucked inside
a hardcover book
she kept beside her bed

∞

synau ysgubo i ffwrdd
spirit of animal or human
enters your spirit at death

∞

synau ysgubo i ffwrdd
strange feeling
of forgetting something
or knowing you know something
not knowing what it is
lingua lethologica

∞

synau ysgubo i ffwrdd
lifting off
leaving the anglo-sphere
lingua englaise behind

∞

synau ysgubo i ffwrdd
cool side of the pillow
on a red-hot airless night

∞

synau ysgubo i ffwrdd
two monks in orange robes
shop at Walmart
in Las Vegas
Super bowl week-end—
wrong

∞

lingua mortuus est
yn iaith marw
it is love
when you find a place to get lost
in a crowd
not noticed, singled out
just to hide alone
surrounded by strangers

words
are figments
of the imagination
to hide behind

∞

hello

y diwedd

Acknowledgements

Thank you to UCalgary Press, and to Aritha Van Herk, for the opportunity to share my poetry as the inaugural book in this new series.

Thank you to Helen Hajnoczky for her many brilliant contributions to the development of this work. Her editorial guidance was astute and unswerving with creative intelligence, and open spirit. Also thanks to Melina Cusano for creating a stunning design for my words to voice from.

Gratitude's to Madelaine Caritas Longman and Shannon Maguire, who took the time to listen to the text and offer their valuable feedback.

The making of this book is connected to *Dragon Rouge*, the recording. My co-producer is the one-and-only Steve Berlin, who brought light to my work as I've never imagined before. And I would like to thank the incomparable Barry Reynolds for his insight and music; and all of the musicians.

Blessed be to Lindsay, Courtney, and Lauren Bell, Lyn Cadence, Margaret Chandler, Romie Christie, Steve Coffey, Lorna Crozier, Jillian Christmas, Kimberley French, Beth Hedva, Bob Holman, Bethan McBreen, Marilyn Milavsky, Kirk Miles, Billeh Nickerson, Mary Pinkoski, Mike Roberts, Julie Trimingham, and Edward Washington for always being there.

"Forest Bathing" was written for a tree planting ceremony created by The Intercultural Dialogue Institute at UCalgary in 2016. "Interview with Ocean" was presented in a 2015 series entitled "Spoken Word Women" at www.thepostfeministpost.com.

About the Author

Award winning author Sheri-D Wilson has published eleven books, created four short films, and released three albums which combine music and poetry. She is known for her electric performance-style, which has made her a fan favorite at festivals around the world. She has read, performed, and taught at festivals across Canada, the United States, the United Kingdom, France, Spain, Belgium, Mexico, and South Africa.

In her poems, Wilson uses personal narrative to address themes of social justice, lost languages, bullying, and violence against women and the earth. Her tenth collection of poetry—*Open Letter: Woman against Violence against Women*—was short-listed for the Robert Kroetsch Poetry Book Award and the CanLit Award. Her collection, *Re:Zoom* (2005), won the Stephan G. Stephansson Award for Poetry. She is editor of the celebrated work *The Spoken Word Workbook: Inspiration from Poets Who Teach*.

Her work has received national and international acclaim with such honours as: City of Calgary Arts Award (2015) * Writer-In-Residence at Kwantlen University (2015) * Feature interview with

Canadian icon Shelagh Rogers (2013) * Featured in Chatelaine Magazine * TED Talk (2012) * Named one of the top ten poets in Canada by CBC (2009) * Subject of a half-hour documentary called Heart of a Poet (2006) * Woman of Vision Award (2006) * SpoCan Poet of Honour (2005) * USA Heavyweight (2003) * Ace Award and AMPIA awards for best short (2003) * 5 Rosie Nominations (2003) * 5 Jessie Nominations (1991).

Sheri-D Wilson is a strong advocate for social change, and is dedicated to fostering artistic communities. In 2016 she produced The School of Thought: Languages Lost & Found, a non-hierarchical gathering of learning and spoken word.

She was Artistic Director of the Calgary Spoken Word Festival from 2003-2014. Sheri-D Wilson was founder and director of the Spoken Word Program at the Banff Centre for Arts and Creativity, 2005-2012.

Follow the ⟳ from the pages of *The Book of Sensations* to Sheri-D Wilson's website to hear her perform the poems

Dreaming in Lost Language
Love Letters
Re: Wyrd
Forest Bathing
The Colour of Ruby
Drones Kill

www.sheridwilson.com

Brave & Brilliant Series

SERIES EDITOR:
Aritha Van Herk, Professor, English, University of Calgary
ISSN 2371-7238 (Print) ISSN 2371-7246 (Online)

Brave & Brilliant publishes fiction, poetry, and everything in between and beyond. Bold and lively, each with its own strong and unique voice, Brave & Brilliant books entertain and engage readers with fresh and energetic approaches to storytelling and verse, in print or through innovative digital publication.

No. 1 · **The Book of Sensations**
Sheri-D Wilson